Lex forcia being a sensible address to the Parliament for an act to remedy the foul abuse of children at schools, especially in the great schools of this nation. (1698)

Anon

Early English Books Online (EEBO) Editions

Imagine holding history in your hands.

Now you can. Digitally preserved and previously accessible only through libraries as Early English Books Online, this rare material is now available in single print editions. Thousands of books written between 1475 and 1700 and ranging from religion to astronomy, medicine to music, can be delivered to your doorstep in individual volumes of high-quality historical reproductions.

We have been compiling these historic treasures for more than 70 years. Long before such a thing as "digital" even existed, ProQuest founder Eugene Power began the noble task of preserving the British Museum's collection on microfilm. He then sought out other rare and endangered titles, providing unparalleled access to these works and collaborating with the world's top academic institutions to make them widely available for the first time. This project furthers that original vision.

These texts have now made the full journey -- from their original printing-press versions available only in rare-book rooms to online library access to new single volumes made possible by the partnership between artifact preservation and modern printing technology. A portion of the proceeds from every book sold supports the libraries and institutions that made this collection possible, and that still work to preserve these invaluable treasures passed down through time.

This is history, traveling through time since the dawn of printing to your own personal library.

Initial Proquest EEBO Print Editions collections include:

Early Literature

This comprehensive collection begins with the famous Elizabethan Era that saw such literary giants as Chaucer, Shakespeare and Marlowe, as well as the introduction of the sonnet. Traveling through Jacobean and Restoration literature, the highlight of this series is the Pollard and Redgrave 1475-1640 selection of the rarest works from the English Renaissance.

Early Documents of World History

This collection combines early English perspectives on world history with documentation of Parliament records, royal decrees and military documents that reveal the delicate balance of Church and State in early English government. For social historians, almanacs and calendars offer insight into daily life of common citizens. This exhaustively complete series presents a thorough picture of history through the English Civil War.

Historical Almanacs

Historically, almanacs served a variety of purposes from the more practical, such as planting and harvesting crops and plotting nautical routes, to predicting the future through the movements of the stars. This collection provides a wide range of consecutive years of "almanacks" and calendars that depict a vast array of everyday life as it was several hundred years ago.

Early History of Astronomy & Space

Humankind has studied the skies for centuries, seeking to find our place in the universe. Some of the most important discoveries in the field of astronomy were made in these texts recorded by ancient stargazers, but almost as impactful were the perspectives of those who considered their discoveries to be heresy. Any independent astronomer will find this an invaluable collection of titles arguing the truth of the cosmic system.

Early History of Industry & Science

Acting as a kind of historical Wall Street, this collection of industry manuals and records explores the thriving industries of construction; textile, especially wool and linen; salt; livestock; and many more.

Early English Wit, Poetry & Satire

The power of literary device was never more in its prime than during this period of history, where a wide array of political and religious satire mocked the status quo and poetry called humankind to transcend the rigors of daily life through love, God or principle. This series comments on historical patterns of the human condition that are still visible today.

Early English Drama & Theatre

This collection needs no introduction, combining the works of some of the greatest canonical writers of all time, including many plays composed for royalty such as Queen Elizabeth I and King Edward VI. In addition, this series includes history and criticism of drama, as well as examinations of technique.

Early History of Travel & Geography

Offering a fascinating view into the perception of the world during the sixteenth and seventeenth centuries, this collection includes accounts of Columbus's discovery of the Americas and encompasses most of the Age of Discovery, during which Europeans and their descendants intensively explored and mapped the world. This series is a wealth of information from some the most groundbreaking explorers.

Early Fables & Fairy Tales

This series includes many translations, some illustrated, of some of the most well-known mythologies of today, including Aesop's Fables and English fairy tales, as well as many Greek, Latin and even Oriental parables and criticism and interpretation on the subject.

Early Documents of Language & Linguistics

The evolution of English and foreign languages is documented in these original texts studying and recording early philology from the study of a variety of languages including Greek, Latin and Chinese, as well as multilingual volumes, to current slang and obscure words. Translations from Latin, Hebrew and Aramaic, grammar treatises and even dictionaries and guides to translation make this collection rich in cultures from around the world.

Early History of the Law

With extensive collections of land tenure and business law "forms" in Great Britain, this is a comprehensive resource for all kinds of early English legal precedents from feudal to constitutional law, Jewish and Jesuit law, laws about public finance to food supply and forestry, and even "immoral conditions." An abundance of law dictionaries, philosophy and history and criticism completes this series.

Early History of Kings, Queens and Royalty

This collection includes debates on the divine right of kings, royal statutes and proclamations, and political ballads and songs as related to a number of English kings and queens, with notable concentrations on foreign rulers King Louis IX and King Louis XIV of France, and King Philip II of Spain. Writings on ancient rulers and royal tradition focus on Scottish and Roman kings, Cleopatra and the Biblical kings Nebuchadnezzar and Solomon.

Early History of Love, Marriage & Sex

Human relationships intrigued and baffled thinkers and writers well before the postmodern age of psychology and self-help. Now readers can access the insights and intricacies of Anglo-Saxon interactions in sex and love, marriage and politics, and the truth that lies somewhere in between action and thought.

Early History of Medicine, Health & Disease

This series includes fascinating studies on the human brain from as early as the 16th century, as well as early studies on the physiological effects of tobacco use. Anatomy texts, medical treatises and wound treatment are also discussed, revealing the exponential development of medical theory and practice over more than two hundred years.

Early History of Logic, Science and Math

The "hard sciences" developed exponentially during the 16th and 17th centuries, both relying upon centuries of tradition and adding to the foundation of modern application, as is evidenced by this extensive collection. This is a rich collection of practical mathematics as applied to business, carpentry and geography as well as explorations of mathematical instruments and arithmetic; logic and logicians such as Aristotle and Socrates; and a number of scientific disciplines from natural history to physics.

Early History of Military, War and Weaponry

Any professional or amateur student of war will thrill at the untold riches in this collection of war theory and practice in the early Western World. The Age of Discovery and Enlightenment was also a time of great political and religious unrest, revealed in accounts of conflicts such as the Wars of the Roses.

Early History of Food

This collection combines the commercial aspects of food handling, preservation and supply to the more specific aspects of canning and preserving, meat carving, brewing beer and even candy-making with fruits and flowers, with a large resource of cookery and recipe books. Not to be forgotten is a "the great eater of Kent," a study in food habits.

Early History of Religion

From the beginning of recorded history we have looked to the heavens for inspiration and guidance. In these early religious documents, sermons, and pamphlets, we see the spiritual impact on the lives of both royalty and the commoner. We also get insights into a clergy that was growing ever more powerful as a political force. This is one of the world's largest collections of religious works of this type, revealing much about our interpretation of the modern church and spirituality.

Early Social Customs

Social customs, human interaction and leisure are the driving force of any culture. These unique and quirky works give us a glimpse of interesting aspects of day-to-day life as it existed in an earlier time. With books on games, sports, traditions, festivals, and hobbies it is one of the most fascinating collections in the series.

The BiblioLife Network

GUIDE TO FOLD-OUTS MAPS and OVERSIZED IMAGES

The book you are reading was digitized from microfilm captured over the past thirty to forty years. Years after the creation of the original microfilm, the book was converted to digital files and made available in an online database.

In an online database, page images do not need to conform to the size restrictions found in a printed book. When converting these images back into a printed bound book, the page sizes are standardized in ways that maintain the detail of the original. For large images, such as fold-out maps, the original page image is split into two or more pages

Guidelines used to determine how to split the page image follows:

• Some images are split vertically; large images require vertical and horizontal splits.
• For horizontal splits, the content is split left to right.
• For vertical splits, the content is split from top to bottom.
• For both vertical and horizontal splits, the image is processed from top left to bottom right.

LEX FORCIA:

Being A

Sensible Address

TO THE

Parliament,

FOR AN

ACT

TO

REMEDY

THE

Foul Abuse of Children at SCHOOLS,

Especially, In the Great Schools of this Nation.

Nimium est quod intelligitur.
Quintilian on this Subject.

LONDON:

Printed for *R. C.* and are to be Sold by *Eliz. Whitlock,*
near *Stationers-Hall,* 1698.

Lex Forcia.

MARCUS FORCIUS, Tribune of the People, prefer'd a Law, *That no Roman Citizen should be Beaten with Rods.* That Man should have his Statute Erected by my consent, that can Prefer such a Law, against the Abuse of them, for the great Schools of this Nation. In the Year 1669. these ensuing Papers for the most part, not altogether (for there are many *Passages* intermingled, not before in *them*, some changed, some left out) were Printed in a little Book in *Duodecimo*, and Licensed by *Roger Le Strange*, they being brought him by a *Knight* of his Acquaintance, and the Book was Presented by a Lively Boy (with a Servant of that *Knight* attendnig him) to the *Speaker*, and to several *Members* of the *House*, as a *Petition* in behalf of the *Children* of this *Nation*; a Quantity of them being paid for, and Designed to that End.

It was not long after that Fine Boy Dyed, and it was an Errand worth his sending into the World if he had Obtained a Consideration of

the

the Matter by the Wiſdom of a Houſe of ſo many *Choice Perſons* as ſtill are *there*, and their *Debate* about it, whatſoever had been the Effect.

One of the *Members*, and an *Active Gentleman*
and *Schollar*, had the Thoughts (if not a Reſolu-
tion) to make a Motion in Regard to the *Petition*, or purpoſe of it : But thinking it wiſe to
Conſult with that Doctor at *Weſtminſter* School,
with whom he had Converſation, it was a wrong
Box he went to, and it is no Wonder if one ſo
much Concern'd (though there was not the leaſt
mention of him then in the Book) ſhould effectu-
ally diſwade him from it.

He was a very Ingenuous Man, and of Great
Vertue, and Publick Spirit, who had one of the
Books ſent him, and wrote back theſe Words : *I
Received the Pretty Book, I hugely like the Deſign
of It, and as much fear thy Prognoſticks of Its Suc-
ceſs. The Stupidity of ſome, the Naughtineſs of others,
and Long Prevalency of a Baſe, Wicked, and Inju-
rious Cuſtom, will, I doubt, Deprive the Nation of
that Great Benefit which it Promiſes.*

It is ſome Advantage, therefore, to the People
of this Kingdom, that as we have our *Parliaments*,
our *Parliament Men* are of diverſe Diſpoſitions,
and our *Parliaments* are Diverſe ; ſo that there is
no Grievance which is publick, eſpecially if it be
general, abiding, and affecting Poſterity, if it be
Preſented at one time, and be not laid to Heart ;
it

it may be Reprefented, Confidered, and Redref-
fed at another. Once in *Seven* Years, at leaft, once
in *Four* times *Seven*, one may make a New Tryal.
I will promife the Man who brings in fuch a Bill,
that the Ages to come fhall Blefs him; and the Age
wherein he lives fhall fay of him, *Hic eft.*

There is not any thing hardly of more Moment
in a *Common - Wealth*, than the *Education* of *Children*, and yet there is generally nothing left more
at Random, and befides the Publick Care. It is the
Cuftom ordinarily of our *Schools*, which being received by our Anceftours, and ufed upon their Innocent
Years, (that are not Senfible of their Mafters Vice, or
their own Injury) does pafs uncontrouled, to commit
to a Perfon, who hath got a little *Greek* and *Latin*,
and nothing elfe perhaps to live upon, and fo is chofen
to the Office, (without any Qualification otherwife,
many times, either of real Worth, or Vertuous Life,
it is well if it be but fo much as Sobriety in Age, and
Modeft Inclinations) the Liberty to ufe fuch a kind of
Difcipline over them, as that the Spring-time of Human Life, (which in all other Creatures is left at the
Greateft Freedom to be Sweet and Jocund) is Deflow-
red and Confumed with Bitternefs and Terrour, to
the drying up the very Sap, which fhould Nourifh
their Bodies, and thofe more lively Spirits, which
fhould animate their Minds, in their future Life, to
Brave Actions.

It is Difputed againft the *Stoicks*, who Condemn
all Anger, that fome Paffion is neceffary to the *Cafti-*

B *gation*

gation of *Youth.* So *Lactantius.* But *Plutarch*, in his Tract about *Cohibition of Anger*, hath laid down a Rule of a contrary Import, that Punishment should never be inflicted out of Self-pleasing; but that when a Man is at present moved, he is first to Correct that Perturbation, before he is fit to Punish the Fault of another under his Tuition. *He that is Hungry, useth his Meat according to Nature; but he that Punisheth, ought to be like the Laws themselves, which are not provoked with any desire at all.* So *Seneca.* So *Cicero.* These *Philosophers* speak cleanly, imagining nothing but of the pleasure of *Revenge*; but what would they say of that Punishment which is made to serve a Viler Affection, and which is to be numbred among those ται ἀτιμίας, and those μὴ καθηκοντα not to be Named.

It hath been a nearer Question of Ancient Debate, whether the Beating Children, should be Allowed, about their Books? We should Imbitter to them their Pleasure, and their Sin, that will do them Hurt: But we should Sugar their Learning, that is, for their Good. The Understanding will not be Enlightned, the Memory Healed, or Invention Quickened, with Stripes upon the Flesh. *Quintillian*, that Famous Institutor of Youth, would have Lads Bred up Hard, to Lye on the Boards, to Eat any thing Coarse, but, by no means, to have *Learners Beaten.* There are several Ingenuous Reasons he has: I will set down only these Words of his which he hath at last, and have affected me much: *Jam si minor in deligendis Custodum & Praeceptorum moribus fuit cura, pudet dicere in qua Probra nefandi homines isto caedendi jure abutantur, non*

mo-

morabar in parte hac, Nimium est quod intelligitur. I will not *English* this, because it is the Sore which I am yet even too tender to touch. I wish, methinks, I had some way only by turning up the Soal of my Shoe, (as Sir *Harry Blunt* says, he saw in *Turkey*, a Woman complaining to the Magistrate of her Husband) to Present the Grievance I would have Redressed.

Sir *Philip Sidney*, that Excellent Person, in his *Arcadia*, hath thought good to set forth this Evil (which I mean) to Publick View, and so to Animadversion, we may suppose, and Emendation, under the Person of *Cecropia*, dealing thus with her *Neices: Cecropia* (says he) *imploying her time in using the same Cruelty on* Pamela, *as on Philoclea, her heart grew not only to desire the fruit of Punishing; but, even to delight in punishing them.* This brave modest Gentleman, had observed, belike, this growing Humour in those that use it: But having a Soul, into which so foul a thought never entred as might direct him right into the Cause of it, he expresses this Practise, complaining Tragically of the Cruelty, but searches not to the Rottenness that lyes at the Core of it. Will you have that shrewd Author *Hudibrass* make the Discovery?

The Pedant in the School Boys Breeches
Does claw and curry his own itches.

By this little we need not wonder at *Dionysius*, the Tyrant, who being expulsed his Kingdom, and got to be Master of a School, should choose that Acquist for the more Voluptuous Dominion. Nor that *Busby* that Tranfcending *Rabbi*, (fo Famous for this Geare, as for this Function) fhould not, at King *Charles's* Coming In, be won to change this *Province*, for any other tendered to him by the Higheft Bounty. And, indeed, if there were not fome fuch thing, and that this at the Root, how fhould the moft of Children meet ftill with fuch doings, not only in His School; but almoft in all others, as they have done? How could Men, that have the Face of *Gravity* and *Difcretion*, be fo highly, and fo readily Offended, at all turns, with the *Innocent?* If the Punifhment were not fuffered to be on thofe parts, the Bowels would Yern, and Hands Relent, when the Child is fo little, and the Fault lefs. But here is the *Mifery* and *Plague* above all, That when thofe Appetites, which are *Natural*, have their Ends, and receive a Completion and Redrefs, in the Attaining that End, the Appetite, which is Un-natural, is Infinite; and thefe ftirred Defires having no Current this way, (I fay in Right Nature) to Satisfaction, and a Surceafe, the Torments of the Children, upon this Account, (who look on their *Schools* as *Hell* it felf) have a Cognation, indeed, hereunto in this, that they never have an end of them.

If Punifhment comes from Self-pleafing, then will it not be in Meafure; Then will it not be Juft; Then the Punifher will be glad of a Fault, who attends the Boys Conftruing only for this. The Fault once fprung, the Bird is fiezed, the Flefh made bare, and how does the Jer-Faulcon pearch over it? Again, Then is this Evil Remedilefs to the Sufferer, feeing the

Caufe

Cause of the Punishment lyes in the Punisher, and not in the Punished to Help it. Then further, every Occasion, and no Fault at all, shall be enough for the *Master* to give himself Pleasure. The *Master* is Idle, takes no Pains, and hath no Patience; and the *Boy* is Beaten (this is what is Common, and Excusable in Comparison) to make Amends, for his own Negligence and Sloth. Then, moreover, shall the Innocent, who are Little Ones, and not able to Conceive of the Matter, be thus Intollerably Miserable, as to be brought almost to their *Wits-End*; and ready to make away themselves, rather than endure the Iteration of those Stripes, whereof they see no Reason, nor hope a Discharge. Then, lastly, must their Torments (I have said already) be, indeed, like those of *Hell*, and no other, seeing they arise from an Unquenchable Fire, in the Appetite of their *Master*.

Not but there have been some *Masters*, and *Dames*, of that Ingenuity and Modesty, as they could never once find in their Hearts, to use this sort of Punishment, to any they ever brought up. Nor but there are some others, who have taken up the Common Usage without Reflection, and their Hearts cannot Reproach them, that they have ever Exercised it from any Instigation whereof they should be ashamed; but only out of Righteousness for their Schollars sake, in Amendment of their Manners, and as they have received the Mistake, (for that, *Quintilian* says, makes them the Duller) the Quickening them in their Books. It is these few Vertuous Men and Women, Born with such Chast Souls, and so averse to what is Filthy, that,

though

though they have had a Call to this Office, could never yet so much as believe, that any other *Masters* or *Mistresses* do such things as they themselves never do, nor thoughton, that is, the Correcting any Child for their Pleasure, but for the Childs Profit only, by whose Severer Vertue and Unbelief this Course is upheld. But when even such as these have heard, or do hear, of our Lewd Sparks Common Prancks in late Days, (imprest, we may suppose, by what they saw first at School) doing thus with the other Sex, their Eyes have opened, or must open, with their Ears, and see what is at the bottom of it. And certainly (I must needs say) for an Accidental Loose *Gentleman*, to be Tempted once or twice to the Using this Sport, while their Whores are at liberty to endure but so much as they list, it is not half so Damn'd a Mischief, as for the *Masters* and *Dames* doing the same Wickedness, with the adding the Hypocrisie, Lye, and Mask of a pretended Justice, Righteousness, and that Holy Thing Discipline, in the doing.

There is a Play called, Sir *Martin Marr-all*, where Sir *John* some-body, being set out in the Humour of Courting only the Simple and Silly Lasses, hath this Passage, *Could I have my Wish, it should be to keep School, and Teach the biggest Girls my self, and here is one in whom my wish is absolved.* This is (or was) a Passage, I thought, enough to puzzle a *Classis* of *Ministers*, or *Bench* of *Justices*: But when it was so commonly Talkt on, when that Play was in Vogue, what I said but now, how the Gallants served their Wenches, even as the *Fryers* used to do their *Nuns*,

As *Gill* his Maid *Gillian* ; As *Tully* tells of *Stilpo* ; and As the *Russian* Women (if *Barclay*, in his *Icon animorum*, and others, do say true) do meafure the love of their Husbands (*Horum in se benevolentiam ex verberum numero æstimant*): It will not be hard to guefs their meaning. Hence the Old Country Ufe, in fome places kept up, of Decking the Bridal Bed, with Sprigs of *Rofemary*, not thinking any further of it, but that it is Comely, or Lucky.

Indeed, a Man cannot fpeak without Shame, and go to expofe this Malady to Cure, (which is the fole end of faying any thing) unlefs by fuch Inftances, as may leave no Man in doubt, but that there is fuch an *Evil*, and that *Evil* ought to be Redrefs'd.

I look on *Numa*, among the *Romans*, who was the Inftitutor of their Religion, to be one of the Pureft *Athiefts* that ever was. This Man did Invent his Order of *Veftal Virgins*, who, upon a Fault committed, were to be Whip'd by the *High Prieft*, and that muft be with pretence of Darknefs, ftark Naked, but it was himfelf only, befure, that would be the *High Prieft*. By his *Books* found in his *Grave*, feveral *Hundred Years* after his *Death*, wrapt up in two Bundles of Wax, he was found to believe none of his own *Superftition*, which, therefore, after the *Prætor* had Read, the *Senate* commanded to be Burnt.

It is not unknown how the *Jefuites*, Govern their *Schools* beyond the *Seas*, nor what they have delivered, fome of them, on this matter, in their Cafes of Confcience.

fcience. Neither would it be any dishonour to us of this Nation, to Change our Customs for better, though we borrowed them from their Example. It cannot, therefore, but be a Wonder to me, that over we should have Parliaments in *England*, and *Westminster* Parliaments, wherein are so many *Gentlemen of Excellent Parts*, and *Ingenious Reflections*, and who, some of them, are not so Old, sometimes, as to forget what they have felt, and seen so little a way off; and yet we never hear of something tendered for the *Regulation* of *Schools*, and what is *Practised* there. Is it because they can, indeed, remember no *Stories*? Or, that the Impressions do yet last that they must not tell *Tales* from thence? And why must not the *Scholar* tell *Tales*? If there were no Confcioufnefs, of what was Ugly in the Fact, What need of *Privacy*? The end of *Vertuous Castigation*, is for *Example*, and such Symptoms do Inform us, That it is not, the *Punished* needs *Amendment*, so much as the *Punisher*; and that the *Punishment* it self needs it most.

As for my own *Education*, when I was yet in Coats, I remember how my *School-Dame*, that Taught me to *Read*, was ready to take her Advantage for this Work. Coming to Learn *Latin*, I went to the *Free-School*, where I was Born: My *Master* was so wofully addicted to this Trade, that I cannot but remember still, how often he would take his turn out of the *School* on purpose for the *Monitor's* Bill, who was to set down every one that did but stir, or look off his Book in the mean while: Oh! How I did dread then, every time he went out! For, no *Care*,

or *Vigilance*, could keep any from *Fault*, when he
defigned to have one found. I cannot but Reflect
how I was ufed, how this Game was followed, and
what Occafion was fought. The *Terrible Life* a poor
Child lives, under fuch a *Mafter*, in regard to the Un-
feen Caufe thereof, is beyond Expreffion, moft *Lamen-
table*.

I will tell how I was ufed one time. My *Mafter*
comes in, (I was a handfom fresh-coloured *Boy*) and
he has a mind: He calls me down, therefore, and
puts me fuddenly on my Leffon : I Fortun'd to difap-
point him, and faid it. But this not cooling him, he
looks all about me, and fees my Stockings, I had on,
New Stockt : *How now !* (fays he) *What Hofe are
here ? Hofe of two colours ?* I told him, (I fuppofe)
They were fuch as my Mother would have me wear.
It is no matter what I faid, this muft be a Crime for
that Occafion, and he ferves his Inclinations. I go
Home, and faid nothing ; but, on the morrow mor-
ning, when the Maid brought me my Stockings to
put on again, I would not endure them. The Maid
tells my Mother ; fhe comes, knowing not the matter, and ufes all means fhe could, fair and foul, yet
would I not wear them. I durft not tell her the Reafon, (for the telling *Tales* out of the *School*, as I have
Intimated, where there is fuch a *School-Mafter*, is made
a worfe Fault than *Treafon*) and my Mother, therefore,
was exceedingly moved at me, as a moft obftinate,
perverfe *Boy* ; having thenceforth her mind eftran-
ged, and retaining the impreffion, fo that fhe was
very near to have got my Father to give away a piece
of Land from me. Which I Recount only to

fhew

ſhew What un-imaginable *Effects* may Ariſe from ſo *Secret* and *Dark* an *Original.*

I muſt Recite yet, with much more Compaſſion, what a Young Gentleman was telling me of a Brother of his, a Spruce, Generous, Brave Spirited *Lad,* whom his Father, therefore, thinking to make him ſo much a more Perfect *Scholar,* takes him from a *Maſter* where he had been cocker'd, and puts him to *Weſtminſter* School. The Young Gentleman coming to ſee, and feel, what doings was there, is not long under the Regiment of that *Doctor,* but his Spirits are Cow'd, his Parts Loſt, and he Returns a *Mope* Home. Shall I tell you of ſome of another Temper? Some Young *Scanderbegs,* in their Reſentment, who, out of Deteſtation of ſuch *Horrid Uſage* as this, did get their Piſtols, and if they had not chanced to Reveal their Intent to ſome of their Fellows, had certainly been their Maſter's Death. Shall I tell of Multitudes, that, not able to Undergo ſuch *Daily Torment,* have fallen to *Truanting,* then to *making Excuſes to their Parents,* then to *Ill Company,* and ſo to have been undone.

Alas! That there ſhould be ſo profound an *Inſenſibility* in *Parents,* who deal with *Children,* as if they were all Born *Mad,* and were to get their *Wits* by *Beating,* or by *ſending them to* Bedlam, which, yet, is far more Eaſy, than to be ſent to ſome *School.*

I remember *Plutarch* tells of *Marius,* who, having ſwoln unhandſom Leggs, calls for a *Chyrurgeon,* and holds

holds forth one of them for him to Launce, and Work upon, as long as he would, not once giving any figh, or with-drawing it, or fpeaking one word: But, when the *Chyrurgeon* had done with that, and call'd for the other, *No,* (fays he) *the Cure is not worth the Pain.* It is true, that *Children,* for the moft part of them, do take their common Lot, and are not able to lay the Thing to Heart, in the Iniquity of it: But fo long as fome of them do, and their *Parents* may, and fhould all do, it is not a little *Greek* and *Latin* for a Gentleman's Son, no, nor all the Hopes of Advantage a Poor Man's Child may have to be of the King's Foundation, (the Hardfhip whereof, to go through, is little known to any but the Poor Lads themfelves) can Compenfate the *Sufferings,* and the *Villany,* they endure.

There are fuch *Stories* that might be told out of *Weftminfter* School, now the Dreadful Venerable *Bard* thereof is Dead, *Eaton* School, *Pauls* School, formerly, and the like Noted Schools, that would make a Heart of Stone to Bleed. There have been *Mafters* Arraigned at Bar for the Death of fome *Boys.* There are *Children* have been ready to Drown themfelves, or make away themfelves, (as before obferved) rather than go to fuch Mafters.

One Boy, in a Country School, being Ripe for the *Univerfity,* tells his *Mafter,* that, on the morrow, his Father would come, and fetch him Home, to carry him thither: The *Mafter* prefently takes him to Task, Pofes him with Queftions, and holding on,

gives

gives him *Forty* Lashes, and upwards, that he might have the Tole of the Grist before it went.

A Grave Person, (one Mr. *Cole*, a *Nonconformist* Minister, in *London*) being a *Westminster* Scholar, had very few less given him at once, by *Busby*, for nothing, but that, upon a False Suppofal, he would not be made to Be-Lye himself, and, when he was ask'd, still stood to the Truth. This *Flagitious Act* was Discover'd to his Friends, by the Maids finding his Shirt all *Bloody*, and his Keeping his Bed. What Stirr came of it afterwards, let himself tell, if any ** Since* that Read this, ask him about it : ** But the *Gentleman*, *this was* that told me of it, but a few Years since, that was then *Writ, this* his *School-Fellow*, received such Horrour at the sight, *Reverend* his *School-Fellow*, received such Horrour at the sight, *Witness is* that the Impreffion of it is never like to go off from *Deceased.* him as long as he lives.

A Woman, that Used to *Teach*, and set Girls to Work, took a Poor Neighbour of mine's Daughter to 'Prentice, and finding some Occasion, *Whips* the Girl, till she was *Stark Dead* ; whereupon, the other Girls crying out, *She was Dead !* *Is she ?* (says the Woman) *I'll fetch her alive again :* And *Whips* on, from the first beginning to the end, a whole Hour by the Clock.

Here are *Masters* and *Dames* fit to be Hang'd ! Butchers, to whom *Calves* should be sent to be Flead, not *Children* to be Instructed ; and yet, How can they
Help

Help themselves, unlefs there be *Bounds* fet upon this *Wickedness* by a *Law?* There is nothing but *An Act of Parliament* about the *Education* of *Children* can deliver the *Nation* from this *Evil*, which I may call the *Kings-Evil*, feeing it is fuch Foundations as theirs, or the like, where there is Provifions made to Breed up Poor Folks Children, (though Vily Converted to fuch as can make moft Friends) and when fuch as depend on this Maintenance are forced to bear any thing rather than be gone ; the other Children yet Free, and Gentlemens Sons, are brought by that means, to undergo the fame *Fate* one with another.

After my firft *School-Mafter*, and another, had left the *School*, a Young *Mafter* was put in, who was a kind of Ingenuous Man, as I had thought, and of another make, but after he came to this Calling, he foon Improves, and Learns the Trick, infomuch that he would fometimes have a Forme of Boys ftand at once with their Breeches down, and Shirts up, or fometimes to go up and down the *School* Bare, and he Slafh them as he pleafed. Oh, there is no Man, if once turn'd *Pedant*, is to be trufted with fuch a fort of Power as this. Such Unclean Temptation muft not be committed to the Vertue or Temperance of a *Socrates* himfelf, which the Tribe of thefe Men (for ought I fee) do take as eafily, as the Boys that come together, do the *Itch* of one another.

I fpoke one time to a *School-Mafter* fomething open, to try if it were fo, as to him, and he anfwered me prefently, *Rogues all, Rogues all.* To my faying to another, *It is* ἀισχρὸν τι. he returned as foon, *It is* 'Δισχιστον. Another turn'd out of his *School* upon this Account, did with a down-caſt ſenſibleneſs bewail the Permiſſion.

And what is the *Reaſon* then for all this, that all this while there is no *Redreſs* of this *Grievance* ſought and effected? Why the *True Reaſon* mainly is this Caution, which the *Wiſe* are apt to conceive within themſelves, that the Reprehending and Speaking of the Thing, and endeavour to Reform it, will put that into ſome ones Head which before they thought not of, and ſo they ſhall Beget and Encreaſe the *Evil* more, inſtead of Extinguiſhing it. But this I take to be certainly that very piece of *Cunning* whereby the *Devil* hath held the World ſo long in this *Vile Practiſe*. The *Ingenuous* forſooth cannot ſpeak of it. A few there be, if they do ſpeak, are afraid it will learn People to be naught, to tell them what is Naught. This is to be acknowledged a Piece of *Sagacity* in ſome Things, but not in this. For theſe few Vertuous Men are miſtaken to think this any ſuch Diſcovery if it be made, that they ſhould need to hide it. Alas! All Men of Reflexion almoſt do know it, having Learn'd it at School by feeling: And yet theſe *Wiſer Men* will think as if they alone did, and ſo won't talk any *Thing* of it. But it is the ſpeaking of the thing, and common exclaiming againſt it, that muſt rid it. For Want of Speaking, the *Evil* is Continued and Encouraged, as Vertuous and Eligible. Beſides, this is one of the Tricks of *Venus* to make a Pleaſure endeared by keeping it private. If it were freely Talkt on, it
would

would lofe its Vigour. Above all, the fpeaking of
it in a *Petition* to the *Parliament*, for *Remedy* of it by
an *Act*, is certainly that way wherein there is no Dan-
ger of Propagation by it. Nay if any (and no *Act*
be) fhould by the Speaking againft it be excited to it,
the Greater Part undoubtedly are liker to be abafhed,
and the Guilty rendered Afhamed by it.

It is not to be forgotten upon this Occafion, how
one, the Scourge, and Scourged of the *Papifts* (I
Name him not, being living) was accufed of *Sodomy*,
(for it was his Life they Thirfted after) when there
was nothing I could ever underftand at the bottom
but this, that he did ufe in keeping Lads to wait on
him to take down their Breeches often, and thrafh
them upon committing any Fault, whereof one or
two of the Greater Ones complained to their Friends,
as that which was Vile to them, and made them leave
his Service, as what they could not abide. Which
Example may Warn thofe that keep Boys and Girls to
Attend them, or be *Taught* by them, to forbear this
Punifhment after they come to their Teens, feeing
Cafuifts who occafionally touch on fuch things, muft
and cannot but Brand it for a *Spice*, or *Degree* of this
Enormity, which is therefore to be Abandoned by
Modeft Perfons.

And here, let all that *Teach School* in the Name of
GOD Examine themfelves. If their Confciences tell
them they are Clear and Clean in this *Thing* it is won-
derful well, for I fear fuch are Rare, or None, if
Noted for *Rigid Mafters.* If Confcience tells themfelves

felves otherwife, that a Delectation there is, and they find it; That they find it and feed it, and in the Exercife of their Function they fulfill daily fuch Defires a; If (I fay) Confcience tells fo, I fee no way for fuch Perfons, but with a Required Shame and Confeffion to quit the calling, for there is no body that lives and dies in a known Sin (this being no Small, I take it, but Vile One) without Repentance (and there can be no *Repentance* where there is no Amendment, and no Amendment when the *Thing* is daily done) can be Saved, according to the Common Sentence of *Divines*, which they themfelves (fome of them being fuch) muft needs know. So much Reafon is there more for an A C T in this *Cafe*, that thofe who are Well-Condition'd Men, and Innocent otherwife, may, with a Safe Confcience, hold their Vocation.

I muft Profefs, it is Grievous to me to have faid any thing of this, if it were not for Confcience fake : I would not be Hired for any Money to Write as I do, that is to Speak fuch Blunt Truth as I do, it is fuch a Penance and *Throws* on my Mind in the Doing, which I would therefore never endure, but for a *Delivery* of the Nation from this *Evil*, that can, never I am fure, without This Means, that is Speaking, be Done.

There

There Remains Two *QUESTIONS* to be Ask'd.

One, What *That Authority*, or *Power* the *Master* hath over the *Schollar* is ? All Power is either *Natural* or *Derived.* The Power of the *Master* is not of Nature, for What hath one Man of himself to do with the Child of another ? The Power which is Derived is either Supream, or Subordinate. The Supream is that which lyes in the Chief Magiftrate, whether it be Derived immediately to him from G O D, or by Confent of the People. The Subordinate is that which is Derived from the Supream to the Inferiour Officers, who Act· in his Name, and from his Authority. The Power of the Mafter now is no fuch Power, neither Deriving from the Magiftrate, or the Laws of the Nation, for he Acts not over the Boys in the K I N G's Name, as the Juftice and the Conftable do. What then is this Adventitious Strange *Power ?* Why this Power the Mafter hath over the Scholar, is that Right of Ruling him which is given him by the Father. It is no Power therefore Supream, but Subordinate ; and not Natural, but Derived from that which is Natural ; and confequently is no other, nor no more, or to any other purpofe than what the

D   Pa-

Parents do allow him. If a Father therefore shall bring his Child to School, and tell the Master, that to preserve the Modesty and Ingenuity of his Spirit, he will never allow this way of Beating him, which is a manifest Prostitution thereof: if the Master shall yet Use it, this Act of the Master is not only Vile, but Unjust, and he is accountable to the Parent for it: Who should therefore either Sue him at Law before some Righteous Judge and Jury to make some body an Example: Or fall upon him with his Cudgel (if he be a Man of Metal) wheresoever he meets him, as having received the First Blow already, on the Flesh of his Child.

The other *QUESTION* is,

What ? Would you then that Children have no Correction at all ?

I say, Yes, and that as Severe as *SOLOMON* himself intends, if clean (such the Parent Allows): When it is meet, and for Vice, or to prevent their being Naught, yet never for their Books, if Disobedience be no Ingredient to it. There should be some Ingenuous Punishments devised by the Master and Dames to shew their Wit and Moderation, which the Children should
tell

tell of when they come home, that their Parents might commend it, and make them love their Schools. There should be an Emulation still enkindled and kept up by Praise and Dispraise, by Getting and Losing the Place. There should be a Substraction of some Play-Game, or Allowed Sport, or Dainty, or some Things the Young Ones hearts are upon, which will Work more with them than these Accustomed Stroaks: Besides, some Training them to Self-denyal, will stand them in Good Stead when they come to Age. For Corporal Sufferings there is the *Ferula* for the Hand, a *Ropes-end* for the Sides, some Drubbing also may be without harm: Nay, some Devices there will be even by Artists quickly in Shops, and as for the *Rod*, which is to be used at last, it is never spoken of in Holy Scripture but for the *Back*. There is no need for making the Boy good, and the Girls good, that the Master or the Dame be made Naught.

I would have no stripes on the Bare, be suffered henceforward to be given any Child out of the House of their Parents (and not there after Twelve) beneath the Waste.

I know here the Diffimulation, and what muft be faid. There is a Neceffity of Caftigation fome-times beyond Reproof, and this is moft Safe, or leaft dangerous, and therefore is chofen and ufed. But this is but One Thing well confidered, & thofe that look but on One Thing in their Deliberations, are eafily miflead. There is more than this One Thing, is, in fo Momentous a Matter as the Inftitu-tion of Youth, to come under Confideration. We may eafily Refolve for the Schollars fecurity, that no Bones be broken, no Boy Maimed or La-med, yet not with the Neglect of Honefty and Vertue.

As for the Training up of our Youth to Good Literature, it is beyond doubt a Noble Thing in its own Nature, and might be an Imployment of Gran-deur for the moft Excellently Born and Qualified, the moft Generous Minds and Braveft Spirits, were it not that this Vitious Sordid Cuftome, and Ill Methods in Teaching, had Difhonoured the Pro-feffion. That Perfon who by Sweetnefs and Gen-tlenefs, or by the Gravity of his Deportment and Countenance, or elfe by Prudence and Contri-vance, is not able to keep a Company of Youth in Order without Violence, is not fit for fuch a Dig-nity as to be *Chofen Præfect* of the Children of a Town, in his admittance to any Publick School, and fo made Ruler over his Hundreds, his Fif-ties, and his Tens.

If.

If there muſt be a *Lictor*, and his bundle be
ſometimes opened, let no Child at any time
be beaten in the Maſter's Heat and Paſſion: If
it be a Fault now, it will be ſo an hour hence:
If it appear not a Crime to morrow, it was
not ſo heinous as he thought it yeſterday. Let
the Boy then undergo a ſolemn kind of Judi-
cature; if it were by a Form of the higheſt
Schollars as Aſſeſſors together with their Maſter, it were but like the *Lacedemonian* Inſtitu-
tion of their Youth, whereof the Chiefeſt Point
lay in this, to enable them to Judge aright of
what was Praiſe-worthy, and what to be Con-
demned in *Human Converſation.* Whatſoever the
Criminal can alledge for himſelf by way of Ju-
ſtification or Extenuation of the Fact, it ought
to be heard with Patience and Candour. If
the Fault cannot be forgiven without Prejudice
to the Community, (*Perſonæ parcendo, ſævitur
in Rempublicam*) let the Doublet be plucked off,
and that part which may Chaſtly lye Naked,
be ſtripped; let the number of the Stripes, according to the Merits of his Delinquency, be
allotted, and the Boy be brought before the
Face of his Maſter for ſeeing juſt Execution.
This is after the manner of the *Hebrew* Judg-
ment, The Malefactor was to lye down before
the Judge, and ſo receive the Stripes appoint-
ed. Let one of the Vileſt Boys then that hath
behaved himſelf worſe of any that day in the
School, be picked out for Executioner, that may

ſerve

ferve for a Shame and Admonition to him, no
lefs than for the juft Suffering of his punifhed Fel-
low.

Our Schools we know, in the *Latin*, are called *Ludi*, *Ludi literarii*, and our Mafters *Ludi
Magiftri*. From whence we muft take the In-
dication, that the Erudition of Children among
the Wifer Ancients, was thought beft to be carry'd on in fuch a way, as that the matters per-
form'd there were made to become in Effect only the Boys *Olympicks*, from which they were
to be kept fometimes as by the Raines, to raife
their minds to Eagernefs, rather than be fpur-
red and gauled to them. There were no need
of the Parents folicitude, or Mafter's blows, to
bring the Boy to Learning, if his Leffons were
but his Recreations, and as fo many Games of
the *Mufes*, unto which he came for his Delight,
and not for Exercife only.

But after all this, before I end, if for fear
of fome unknown Harm to Children by other
Punifhments not in ufe, the Major Vote of the
Wife fhall be for letting this Cuftom ftill ob-
tain, yet muft it needs be very fit that fome
Reformation be made, if not quite as to the
Villany, at leaft as to the Butchery thereof, in
regard to thofe Mafters and Dames that have no
Bowels.

Bowels. It were a Good Thing therefore, if nothing elfe can be done, that thefe Three Things were but confider'd and limited :

The Age of the Schollar,

The Meafure of the Weapon,

And, *The Number of the Stripes.*

When there are thofe fharp long cutting Rods, and Bundles of them made for our great Schools, fuch as not *One* Parent of a *Hundred* would Allow his Child to come under, if he could chufe ; and the tender Mother would fwound almoft to fee one of them : When fuch Preparations as one would think could have been invented only for Torture of the Martyrs, whom they Tormented to Death, have been made for Correction of Poor Children, even for Innocent Matters, Turning our Schools into very Shambles, *Ubi torquentur* (as *Cyprian* has it) *non membra fed vulnera :* Which Practife our Mafters ftill, if it were not for fome of their own Better Natures, might follow : It is time to fay to this Sea, *Hitherto.* What ? Shall the Nation endure a quite Arbitrary Power over our Free-Born Children by a Pedant, when we cannot bear with the leaft part of it over our felves by a King ? Suppofe then it be agreed, that every Lad
after

after *Fourteen*, (and the Female fooner) be En-
franchized from this Punifhment altogether, fo
that from thenceforth it fhall be to them a matter
Obfcene ; and that for thofe under that Age, no
Rod fhall be in Length above fuch a ftint ; (Suppofe but Half the Ell) And no Stripes above
fuch a Number ; (Suppofe but Three) And that if
any Mafter fhall exceed thefe Limits in any of the
Three Particulars, it fhall be prefent Expulfion ;
No Schollar, Old or Young, being exempt from
other Difcipline, according to Defert, otherwife :
I fay, if there were nothing more (though in a
B I L L concerning *The Education of Youth*, many a Thing more would be thought on, and put
in) could be done, fuch an A C T yet would
be a *Good Act* ; and to Compafs it, a very *Worthy
Exploit.*

But, Alas ! Why fhould any be of fo flight confideration, as to think, that Children might not
be Corrected otherwife ? What if an Engine were
invented (as I heard the Ingenuous Dr. *Wilkins*
once fpeaking)to fupply the place of fuch an ill Mafter, whofe Skill to make Schollars is only by Com-
pulfion, as like to prove the better Tool (becaufe
Innocent) for that purpofe, than He ? What if it
were Enacted, *That all Children that go to School
fhall wear Drawers, and that they fhall be never
Whipt but with their Drawers on ?*

To

To CONCLUDE:

It is Humane, it is Religious, it is Fit, that all Inftruction and Caftigation of Children be Holy, and nothing allowed in our Schools but what is conformable to Modefty, to Ingenuity, and Vertue. And confequently that fuch a Ufage to the contrary, which is Bafe, which is Foul, the longer it hath Obtained fhould be the rather Reclaimed : Seeing I muft, moft folemnly now at the end profefs, not only the Thing to be an Evil, but the Greateft Evil I know, or can think, which hath Publick Allowance, of any whatfoever the Sun fees.

An Evil (let me fay on) which is not *Malum trifte* only, (for then it fhould be borne yet for me) but *Malum turpe*. The Corruption of Difcipline: The Bane of all Good Education. The Infection of the School-Mafter: The Difhonour of their Function. The Infandum of the Teacher: The Horrendum of the Taught. The Stupid Man's Idol : A *Tophet* to thofe that have their Eyes open. To the one a Ludicrous Matter: To the other, *An Iniquity to be Punifh'd by the Judges.*

Son of Man, I have fet thee as a Watch-man to the Houfe of Ifrael; *if thou doft not fpeak to Warn the Wicked from his way, that Man fhall*

E *Die*

Die in his Iniquity, but his Blood will I require at thy hand : Nevertheless, if thou warn the Wicked of his way to Turn from it, if he do not Turn from his way, he shall Die in his Iniquity, but thou hast delivered thy Soul.

I know that the World lyes in Wickedness, and if it be Warn'd, and will lye in Wickedness, let it lye. If the Nation will not take the Warning, but will be Wicked, and a *Sodom,* let it be Wicked still. If Parliament after Parliament, and this Parliament will not mend it, let the Wickedness lye on those that can help it : As for my self, I deliver my own Soul. The Trumpet is blown, let the sound thereof go abroad, and those that will, let them know the meaning of it.

FINIS.

Once and again, but Satan hindred.

CPSIA information can be obtained at www.ICGtesting.com
Printed in the USA
BVOW02s1150260814

364295BV00020B/652/P

9 781171 259213